FRANCIS FRITH'S

NORFOLK COAST
PHOTOGRAPHIC
MEMORIES

Happy Christmas Mum,

love

Julia

2012

THE FRANCIS FRITH COLLECTION

www.francisfrith.com

FRANCIS FRITH'S

NORFOLK COAST

PHOTOGRAPHIC MEMORIES

NEIL STOREY is a born and bred Norfolk man. A graduate of the University of East Anglia and one of the foremost historians of the county, he has published over 20 books and countless articles for magazines and journals on a wide variety of regional history topics. Undoubtedly a man blessed with a ready wit and ebullient character, he is a familiar voice on BBC local radio; he has also acted as a consultant and featured on a number of television documentaries and dramas. Neil is in constant demand by both academic and social audiences for his lectures, talks and legendary after-dinner speeches on social and military history topics.

FRANCIS FRITH'S
PHOTOGRAPHIC MEMORIES

NORFOLK
COAST

PHOTOGRAPHIC MEMORIES

NEIL STOREY

First published in the United Kingdom in 2005 by
The Francis Frith Collection

Hardback Edition Published in 2005
ISBN 1-85937-651-7

Paperback Edition ISBN 978-1-84589-416-0

British Library Cataloguing in Publication Data

Norfolk Coast - Photographic Memories
Neil Storey

The Francis Frith Collection
Frith's Barn, Teffont,
Salisbury, Wiltshire SP3 5QP
Tel: +44 (0) 1722 716 376
Email: info@francisfrith.co.uk
www.francisfrith.co.uk

Printed and bound in Great Britain

Front Cover: **WELLS-NEXT-THE-SEA**, *The Quay 1929* 81998t
Frontispiece: **GREAT YARMOUTH**, *The Marina and Britannia Pier c1955* G56042

The colour-tinting is for illustrative purposes only, and is not intended to be historically accurate

Aerial photographs reproduced under licence from Simmons Aerofilms Limited
Historical Ordnance Survey maps reproduced under licence from Homecheck.co.uk

Every attempt has been made to contact copyright holders of illustrative material.
We will be happy to give full acknowledgement in future editions for any items not credited.
Any information should be directed to The Francis Frith Collection.

AS WITH ANY HISTORICAL DATABASE THE FRITH ARCHIVE IS CONSTANTLY
BEING CORRECTED AND IMPROVED AND THE PUBLISHERS WOULD WELCOME
INFORMATION ON OMISSIONS OR INACCURACIES

CONTENTS

FRANCIS FRITH
VICTORIAN PIONEER

FRANCIS FRITH, founder of the world-famous photographic archive, was a complex and multi-talented man. A devout Quaker and a highly successful Victorian businessman, he was philosophical by nature and pioneering in outlook.

By 1855 he had already established a wholesale grocery business in Liverpool, and sold it for the astonishing sum of £200,000, which is the equivalent today of over £15,000,000. Now a very rich man, he was able to indulge his passion for travel. As a child he had pored over travel books written by early explorers, and his fancy and imagination had been stirred by family holidays to the sublime mountain regions of Wales and Scotland. 'What lands of spirit-stirring and enriching scenes and places!' he had written. He was to return to these scenes of grandeur in later years to 'recapture the thousands of vivid and tender memories', but with a different purpose. Now in his thirties, and captivated by the new science of photography, Frith set out on a series of pioneering journeys up the Nile and

to the Near East that occupied him from 1856 until 1860.

INTRIGUE AND EXPLORATION

These far-flung journeys were packed with intrigue and adventure. In his life story, written when he was sixty-three, Frith tells of being held captive by bandits, and of fighting 'an awful midnight battle to the very point of surrender with a deadly pack of hungry, wild dogs'. Wearing flowing Arab costume, Frith arrived at Akaba by camel sixty years before Lawrence of Arabia, where he encountered 'desert princes and rival sheikhs, blazing with jewel-hilted swords'.

He was the first photographer to venture beyond the sixth cataract of the Nile. Africa was still the mysterious 'Dark Continent', and Stanley and Livingstone's historic meeting was a decade into the future. The conditions for picture taking confound belief. He laboured for hours in his wicker dark-room in the sweltering heat of the desert, while the volatile chemicals fizzed dangerously in their trays. Back in London he exhibited his photographs and was 'rapturously cheered' by members of the Royal Society. His reputation as a photographer was made overnight.

VENTURE OF A LIFE-TIME

Characteristically, Frith quickly spotted the opportunity to create a new business as a specialist publisher of photographs. He lived in an era of immense and sometimes violent change.

For the poor in the early part of Victoria's reign work was exhausting and the hours long, and people had precious little free time to enjoy themselves. Most had no transport other than a cart or gig at their disposal, and rarely travelled far beyond the boundaries of their own town or village. However, by the 1870s the railways had threaded their way across the country, and Bank Holidays and half-day Saturdays had been made obligatory by Act of Parliament. All of a sudden the working man and his family were able to enjoy days out and see a little more of the world.

With typical business acumen, Francis Frith foresaw that these new tourists would enjoy having souvenirs to commemorate their days out. In 1860 he married Mary Ann Rosling and set out on a new career: his aim was to photograph every city, town and village in Britain. For the next thirty years he travelled the country by train and by pony and trap, producing fine photographs of seaside resorts and beauty spots that were keenly bought by millions of Victorians. These prints were painstakingly pasted into family albums and pored over during the dark nights of winter, rekindling precious memories of summer excursions.

THE RISE OF FRITH & CO

Frith's studio was soon supplying retail shops all over the country. To meet the demand he gathered about him a small team of photographers, and published the work of independent artist-photographers of the calibre of Roger Fenton and Francis Bedford. In order to gain some understanding of the scale of Frith's business one only has to look at the catalogue issued by Frith & Co in 1886: it runs to some 670 pages, listing not only many thousands of views of the British Isles but also many photographs of most European countries, and China, Japan, the USA and Canada - note the sample page shown on page 9 from the hand-written Frith & Co ledgers recording the pictures. By 1890 Frith had created the greatest specialist photographic publishing company in the world, with over 2,000 sales outlets - more than the combined number that Boots and WH Smith have today! The picture on the next page shows the Frith & Co display board at Ingleton in the Yorkshire Dales (left of window). Beautifully constructed with a mahogany frame and gilt inserts, it could display up to a dozen local scenes.

POSTCARD BONANZA

The ever-popular holiday postcard we know today took many years to develop. In 1870 the Post Office issued the first plain cards, with a pre-printed stamp on one face. In 1894 they allowed other publishers' cards to be sent through the mail with an attached adhesive halfpenny stamp. Demand grew rapidly, and in 1895 a new size of postcard was permitted called the court card, but there was little room for illustration. In 1899, a year after Frith's death, a new card measuring 5.5 x 3.5 inches became the standard format, but it was not until 1902 that the divided back came into being, so that the address and message could be on one face and a full-size illustration on the other. Frith & Co were in the vanguard of postcard development: Frith's sons Eustace and Cyril continued their father's monumental task, expanding the number of views offered to the public and recording more and more places in Britain, as the coasts and countryside were opened up to mass travel.

Francis Frith had died in 1898 at his villa in Cannes, his great project still growing. The archive he created continued in business for another seventy years. By 1970 it contained over a third of a million pictures showing 7,000 British towns and villages.

FRANCIS FRITH'S LEGACY

Frith's legacy to us today is of immense significance and value, for the magnificent archive of evocative photographs he created provides a unique record of change in the cities, towns and villages throughout Britain over a century and more. Frith and his fellow studio photographers revisited locations many times down the years to update their views, compiling for us an enthralling and colourful pageant of British life and character.

We are fortunate that Frith was dedicated to recording the minutiae of everyday life. For it is this sheer wealth of visual data, the painstaking chronicle of changes in dress, transport, street layouts, buildings, housing, engineering and landscape that captivates us so much today. His remarkable images offer us a powerful link with the past and with the lives of our ancestors.

THE VALUE OF THE ARCHIVE TODAY

Computers have now made it possible for Frith's many thousands of images to be accessed almost instantly. Frith's images are increasingly used as visual resources, by social historians, by researchers into genealogy and ancestry, by architects and town planners, and by teachers involved in local history projects.

In addition, the archive offers every one of us an opportunity to examine the places where we and our families have lived and worked down the years. Highly successful in Frith's own era, the archive is now, a century and more on, entering a new phase of popularity. Historians consider the Francis Frith Collection to be of prime national importance. It is the only archive of its kind remaining in private ownership. Francis Frith's archive is now housed in an historic timber barn in the beautiful village of Teffont in Wiltshire. Its founder would not recognize the archive office as it is today. In place of the many thousands of dusty boxes containing glass plate negatives and an all-pervading odour of photographic chemicals, there are now ranks of computer screens. He would be amazed to watch his images travelling round the world at unimaginable speeds through internet lines.

The archive's future is both bright and exciting. Francis Frith, with his unshakeable belief in making photographs available to the greatest number of people, would undoubtedly approve of what is being done today with his lifetime's work. His photographs depicting our shared past are now bringing pleasure and enlightenment to millions around the world a century and more after his death.

9

NORFOLK COAST
AN INTRODUCTION

ALTHOUGH I HAVE NOT travelled the world, I am convinced there is nowhere I would rather live than the Norfolk coast. This is a place of outstanding natural beauty, be it the sweeping open vistas of the West Norfolk coast, the creeks of the Burnhams, the salt marshes of Salthouse and Cley, the heights of Weybourne, or the gently undulating coastline of dunes and marrams around Sea Palling and Winterton. The freedom you feel when beneath those great open skies, and the ability to observe the changing seasons and to literally live and breathe the Norfolk coast, is truly a privilege and an experience to treasure in your heart and soul. Judging by the longevity of many of the local folk around here, it has got to be good for you too!

For those who earn a living from the sea, it is not an easy life. The rich fruits yielded to crab and lobster pots or the harvests of shellfish must be tempered with the dangers of the sea and the toll she claims in life and land every year. Norfolk's lifeboats and their brave crews are renowned

BLAKENEY, *The Quay c1955* B121045

across the country. In their 112 years of service, RNLI boats at Caister have saved 1814 lives, a total unequalled by any other station. Henry Blogg, 'one of the bravest lifeboatmen that ever lived', was awarded the George Cross, the British Empire Medal, the RNLI Gold Medal three times, and four Silver Medals; he served 53 years on the Cromer lifeboats, 38 of them as Coxswain. He and his brave crews were responsible for the saving of 873 lives. The awards for bravery that lifeboat crews along the coast still quietly and modestly receive reflect the dangers of the waters of this coast today.

The sea has claimed a lot of the old coastline of Norfolk. Whole towns and villages have steadily fallen beneath the waves as year by year more of the cliffs are eaten away; sometimes the occasional high seas and storms bite a whole chunk away. Towns like Eccles and Whimpwell have been reduced to a scattering of houses built years after the original settlement. Nothing is left of Shipden, the town that once stood to the seaward side of Cromer, although old fishermen claimed that they would not go to sea if they heard the submerged bells of Shipden church booming beneath the waves—there would be a bad storm brewing!

This book is divided into four chapters that quarter the coastline and reflect the unique features and character of each area. We begin our journey far round to the west with the ancient port of King's Lynn; we travel through its neighbours to the resort of New Hunstanton, the vision of Henry Styleman le Strange from the 1840s. Then we go through the Burnhams, an attractive group of seven parishes known today as Burnham Deepdale, Norton, Overy, Sutton, Thorpe, Ulph, and Market (or Westgate).

The tragedy here, and to greater and lesser extents right along the North Norfolk coast, is that a large number of properties have become second homes only occupied for a few months or weeks of the year, and some of the villages in this area appear almost depopulated during the winter months. The prices of these desirable homes have rocketed over recent years, and local youngsters find it almost impossible to get on the housing ladder in the town or village where their family have lived for years. Because of this, local 'characters' and the whole persona of coastal villages are under threat. The number of incomers to the Burnhams over recent years has provoked concern and debate to the degree that it has been nick-named 'Chelsea on Sea'.

The Burnhams is an area beloved of sailors ancient and modern. Many of us have enjoyed days sailing or rowing around the creeks of Overy Staithe. Here is the cradle of a number of naval heroes. The great 18th-century admirals Sir John Narborough and Cloudesley Shovell were local men who knew these waters well; but above all, this is Nelson country. Our greatest naval commander was born at Burnham Thorpe, and learned to sail on the waters around here. On the fringes of the Burnhams begins the massive Holkham Estate, home to successive Earls of Leicester since 1734. Thanks to their benevolence and foresight, much of this part of the coastline has been stabilised by the planting of Corsica pines. The Holkham dunes are England's largest designated National Nature Reserve: covering over 10,000 acres, it spans 9 miles between Burnham Overy and Blakeney.

Our second chapter runs from Wells to Weybourne. Here were once the considerable Glaven ports of Wells, Blakeney, Cley, Salthouse and Stiffkey. After embankments to stop flooding were erected by Dutch engineers in the 17th century, the sea began to erode them; it took the sands and gravels of the embankments into the channels and silted up the entrances to the ports, literally choking them to death. The larger trading ships were unable to navigate into the harbours without groundings or difficulties in these clogged channels. Almost as if to spite these villages further for their defiance, the sea has subsequently breached what defences were left and flooded the salt marshes - or in extreme cases, such as the 1953 floods, has smashed into the villages themselves.

The third chapter embraces 'Poppyland'. Inspired by the ruined tower of Sidestrand church, which perched precariously on the edge of the cliff surrounded by gravestones and poppies, Clement Scott called it 'The Garden of Sleep'; he waxed lyrical over this area, which he called 'Poppyland', in his regular features for the Daily Telegraph in the 1880s and 90s. It captured many imaginations, and soon trains were coming direct from London to Cromer carrying thousands who wanted to stay or visit this magical land for themselves. Poppies swayed in the fields beyond Cromer, and the coastal hamlet of Sheringham soon enjoyed the benefits of the holiday trade, and so did the other villages and hamlets in this area that received the overflow and passing trade of the Poppyland phenomenon.

In the final chapter we explore the gentle coastline of marrams and dunes between Paston, Great Yarmouth and Gorleston. Situated beyond the railways which brought the Poppyland traffic, many of these settlements relied on the fishing trade for much longer than their North-East Norfolk counterparts. Sea Palling and Horsey have been shaped by the sea. Today coastal management and the tourist trade are the mainstays of these villages, but they have paid a hard price over the years from encroachments by the sea. Acres of land around Horsey were stained a sickly rust brown and rendered useless for years after the sea breached the coastline here in February 1938, flooding over 15 square miles of farms and marshes. Far worse were the floods on the night of Saturday 31 January and Sunday 1 February 1953, when hurricane winds and a tidal surge smashed onto the east coast of Britain. Every one of our coastal towns was damaged. The disaster at Sea Palling saw seaward residences reduced to rubble, wrecked, and flooded out. Seven people died here. The effect on village people was profound.

Our journey concludes on the stretch of 'holidayland' between Hemsby, Caister and Great Yarmouth. In the 1930s commentators wrote disparagingly of the line of wooden bungalows which peppered this area of coastline, decrying the 'pleasures' of sand blowing between the slats and sitting in poorly furnished accommodation heated by and filled with the smell of paraffin stoves. Since the 1950s Hemsby has developed concrete holiday centres surrounded by barbed wire and its own 'golden mile' of amusement arcades.

At Caister, an ancient settlement with fascinating Roman remains, we find the father of all holiday camps, for it is here that one Fletcher Dodd opened a 'socialist camp' in 1906 for people of that political persuasion from the grimy East End of London to come and stay for a break. He soon saw the potential of the idea, and acquiring nearby land, he founded the first holiday camp in England. In its heyday the camp had its own railway halt, and 'holiday camp expresses' stopped there en route from London to Great Yarmouth.

In Great Yarmouth and Gorleston we complete our journey. Unlike King's Lynn, which remained predominantly a port, Great Yarmouth was able to embrace the functions of both port and holiday destination, with its harbour channel to the west and its holiday resort facing out east across the North Sea. Begun with a spa and bath house in the 18th century, the holiday trade in the town grew apace from the mid-19th century, when the resort was to become the first Norfolk coastal town to obtain a railway link. Seafront terraces and development grew apace from the 1840s, and soon the Wellington Pier

(1854) and Britannia Pier (1858) were stretching their airy promenades out to sea; a tradition of entertainment innovations, attractions and ornamental gardens was begun in the town.

It has been a pleasure to select these wonderful images from the Frith archives to relate some of the story of the Norfolk coast. History is like digging in ancient sand hills—the more you dig, the more you find. Take your time to look at these nostalgic images; the clarity and details are remarkable, and I am convinced they will stir nostalgic memories or fascinate the reader by revealing a compelling portrait of the Norfolk coast in the past. They are all timely reminders of how much has changed, and of how much of the past we have left today. I hope it will inspire us all to look after it for future generations.

GREAT YARMOUTH, *The Sands from Britannia Pier 1922* 72514

KING'S LYNN *from the air 1975* AF310912

KING'S LYNN
TO HOLKHAM

KING'S LYNN, *The Quay 1898* 40893

Pictured on a quiet day, this picturesque quayside area beside the seaborne channel of the Ouse has seen almost unbroken trade for a thousand years. In the late 19th century the main trade here would have been from tall-masted trading vessels delivering cattle foods and taking coal, corn, sand and an array of locally produced goods in return.

KING'S LYNN
The Custom House
c1955 K28018

The Custom House is a memorial to the importance and value of sea trade to King's Lynn. Built by Sir John Turner as an exchange for merchants in 1683, it was purchased by the Crown for a Custom House in 1715. The father of George Vancouver (1757-98), the man who acquired British Columbia for the nation, was a customs officer here.

KING'S LYNN, *Red Mount 1891* 28755

Situated in St James's Park is the octagonal Red Mount Chapel, erected atop the mound in 1484 and dedicated to 'Our Ladye of the Mount'. It was popular with pilgrims, who visited it on their way to or from the shrine of Our Lady at Walsingham. It fell into dilapidation after the Dissolution in c1540, and its lower apartment was reduced to a stable; it was restored to its former glory by the corporation in the 19th century.

▶ **KING'S LYNN**
Nelson Street 1908
60025

To the left of the photograph we can see the gable of the Valiant Sailor public house, which abutted with Priory Lane. Trade was brisk here, for sailors approaching from South Quay saw this hostelry before all others, and there were about 400 pubs to choose from in the town in the 19th century! This area was rife with 'hoares and harpies', and fights and smash-ups were frequent; it is hardly surprising that Read & Wilbur, the builders and undertakers on the right, were kept in business for many a year.

◀ **KING'S LYNN**
Norfolk Street 1891
28769

In the late 19th century this area of Norfolk Street offered such delights as Mrs Elizabeth Cockerill, china, glass and earthenware dealer, Plowright & Pratt (extreme right), ironmongers by appointment to the Prince of Wales, who sold iron bars, rods, hoops and sheets, the Singer Sewing Machine Manufacturing Company, and John Devonshire (fourth shop from the left), fishmonger, mineral water manufacturer and fish manure dealer!

▲ **SNETTISHAM,** *Queen Alexandra's Bungalow 1908* 61116

The bungalow was situated on the beach for the convenience of Her Majesty. She often visited on summer days with her entourage of servants and guests. Sad to say, it became storm-damaged, fell into disrepair and was eventually demolished.

◀ **SNETTISHAM**
The Old Hall c1955 S464013

The hall dates from the early 16th century, when Wymond Cary leased the estate from the Crown. Remodelled with gables in c1625, the hall passed to the Styleman family in 1710, who made many alterations. In 1877 the hall was sold again, and then began a chequered existence of rentals and military occupation in wartime. The last family to occupy the hall as their home between the 1930s and 70s were the Stricklands, notably General Sir Peter Strickland, the longest serving colonel of the Royal Norfolk Regiment. The Hall was sold after his widow's death in 1977 to become a Sue Ryder Home.

► **HEACHAM**
The Church and the War Memorial 1921
71049

The 15th-century church, dedicated to St Mary, contains a number of memorials to the wealthy local family of Rolfe. Among their number was John Rolfe of Heacham Hall, who married the Indian princess Pocahontas and brought her to England in 1616. An alabaster memorial to her was erected in the church in 1933.

◄ **HEACHAM**
High House c1955
H57001

Built about 1726, in the early 20th century High House was a co-educational boarding school founded by Harry Lowerinson. In 1926 it was taken over by the Workers Travel Association and used as holiday accommodation until the Second World War, when it became a billet for Polish troops. Reverting to holiday accommodation after the war it fell into disrepair, and its grounds were used for housing development in the mid 1970s.

▲ **HEACHAM,** *North Beach c1965* H57112

Heacham has the distinctive flat beach of this part of the West Norfolk coast. There could be no harbour, so only coal vessels and small sea-going craft ever unloaded their cargoes on the sand here. Over the last 100 years, Heacham has become popular among those seeking a quieter, less commercial seaside destination.

◄ **HUNSTANTON**
The Cliffs from the South 1896 38410

These cliffs are distinctive and unique along the Norfolk coast. The base is carrstone of a dark brown tint below and yellow above. On this rests a band of bright red chalk, and above it is white chalk, which forms the upper part of the cliff face.

▼ **HUNSTANTON,** *The Parade 1891* 28772

Hunstanton is pictured here while the town was still under construction: note that on the right of the photograph there is no Town Hall. What does exist at this date is the Golden Lion Hotel, the first building to be erected in New Hunstanton. Folks who did not believe in Henry Styleman le Strange's vision for a seaside resort on this site christened it 'le Strange's Folly'.

► **HUNSTANTON**
The Beach 1907 58892

Viewed from the pier, on the left is the Sandringham Hotel (now demolished), built by the Great Eastern Railway for the thousands of visitors it brought to the town at the turn of the century. In front of the hotel the promenade and sea defences can be seen under construction.

HUNSTANTON
From the Pier 1907
58897

The pier was erected in 1870. Supported on cast iron columns built on screw piles, it extended some 800ft in length and was described at the time of the photograph as affording 'a spacious landing-place and an agreeable promenade ... where the air is known to be strongly impregnated with ozone'.

HUNSTANTON
The Green 1921 71020

Here on the Green those visitors who did not wish to dabble on the sands with Punch and Judy, minstrels and organs could enjoy the relative peace of this area to read, write a postcard or two, have a picnic or await the return of their charabanc to take them home.

► **HUNSTANTON**
The Cross and the Pier
1921 71021

When Henry Styleman le
Strange constructed New
Hunstanton he wanted
to give the resort some
character, so he installed the
Cross (right). Its true origins
are unclear, but the most
feasible suggestion is that
it was the old market cross
of Snettisham, which the le
Strange family brought to
Old Hunstanton when they
inherited the estates, and
had it installed here when
the new town was founded.

◄ **HUNSTANTON**
The Pier 1921 71033

The pier is seen here in its heyday, complete with its Mikado Concert Hall erected at its head in 1912. On the left, local fishermen with their boats and horse-drawn cart are landing their catch. The fine white-sailed boat out at sea was a holiday boat, which would take visitors on a little trip around the pier and along the beach.

▼ **HUNSTANTON,** *The Beach from the Pier 1927* 79727

This crowded beach beautifully illustrates the beach fashions of the 1920s: ladies wear summer dresses with straw hats, while the boys and gentlemen retain flat caps, jackets and trousers (rolled up if they fancied a paddle!). Only a few of the youngsters are adventurous enough to wear swimming suits.

► **HUNSTANTON**
The Swimming Pool c1965
H135118

This open air bathing pool was constructed between 1924 and 1928 on land reclaimed by the construction of the sea wall. Opened with due ceremony in 1928, this pool and the nearby ornamental gardens and boating lake have all disappeared today to make way for car parks, caravan sites and modern entertainment centres.

HUNSTANTON
The Beach and the Pier c1955 H135067

This view shows the full extent of the 800ft pier. After surviving a fire in September 1934 it was restored, but it was not as well maintained as it might have been. Dilapidated by the end of the 1960s, it was badly damaged by a storm in 1978, and most of what remained was destroyed by local authority order in 1979. Nothing of the pier remains today.

HUNSTANTON
The Pier Skating Rink c1965 H135115

One of the fads of entertainment which has come in and out of vogue since Victorian times has been roller skating. Here on the pier skates could be hired, or you could bring your own, and you could skate around to your heart's content. There was even a small supply of cushions that could be tied on to the behinds of inexperienced adults in the event of their skidding over.

HUNSTANTON
Manor Park Caravan Site c1965 H135127

After the disastrous floods of 1953 had passed, and the wrecked pre-fab houses near the south beach were cleared away, the holiday trade filled the void. The distinctive rows of bright white-topped caravans and mobile homes occupied the site.

HUNSTANTON, *Manor Park Larder, Manor Park Caravan Site c1965* H135139

From the early days of caravan parks, it soon became apparent that visitors wanted the sites to become 'one stop shops' incorporating shopping and entertainment. Often sites would also have small restaurants, milk bars and even hair salons.

HUNSTANTON
*The Garden of Rest
1929* 81933

The gardens were laid out in memory of the local fallen of the First World War. On the left are the ruins of St Edmund's Chapel, erected in 1272; it was built near the site where Edmund, the Martyr King, was supposed to have landed in AD 855 to be crowned King of East Anglia. The chapel was used for worship until the 16th century; just the ruinous arch remains today.

HUNSTANTON, *The Lighthouse 1898* 40901

The lighthouse was built by Trinity House in 1844; the occulting light at the top of its 50ft tower could be seen up to 16 miles out to sea. When the lighthouse ceased operations in 1921 the light was removed, and the tower became refreshment rooms, and subsequently a gunnery and observation station during the Second World War. Sold in 1996, it can now be hired as a holiday home.

OLD HUNSTANTON
The Church 1893 32271

This is a view beloved of generations of artists and photographers. The church of St Mary the Virgin was built in the 14th century. Generations of the Le Strange family have been buried here, and their memorials festoon the walls and floor. It is also members of this family who have rescued the church from ruin on two occasions.

31

▶ **OLD HUNSTANTON**
The Neptune Hotel
c1960 O119102

There has been a beer house in the village for well over 200 years. The innkeepers were not choosey over how they obtained their spirits, and there was a great smuggling trade here. Monuments to the brave officers who attempted to stem the trade in contraband still stand in the church yard: these are William Green, a customs officer, and Light Dragoon William Webb, who were both killed by smugglers in 1784.

◀ **HUNSTANTON**
Old Elms, Ringstead Down 1896 38414

This spot is beloved of tobogganers in the snow and strollers the rest of the year. The air here was said to be of a very fine quality, and the wells sunk deep in the chalk hereabouts were said to provide finer water than that of the spa at Harrogate.

▲ **BURNHAM OVERY STAITHE,** *The Creek c1955* O80006

Pictured from the Hard, with old maltings on the left, this peaceful view cannot be easily replicated today, as the ground here fills up with cars in the summer months and sailing boats battened down for the bad weather in the winter time.

◄ **BURNHAM OVERY STAITHE**
The Creek c1955 O80009

Here the Burn winds its way through lavender-covered salt marshes to the sea; here the sand dunes stretch away to Holkham in the east and Scolt Head island to the west. A number of the boats here were still working boats at this date; fishermen took them out to sea to mussel beds renowned for the size and quality of their shellfish.

► **BURNHAM MARKET**
The Village c1955
B500001

On the green is the war memorial to the fallen of the First World War which was unveiled with due ceremony by Lord Leicester in the 1920s. To the right of the memorial may be seen the drapery shop kept for many years by Mr Daniel Searle.

◄ **BURNHAM MARKET**
The Village c1955
B500007

This view takes in the east end of the Market Place and Front Street. On the right is G W Roy's fancy repository and the post office, and just beyond that is the Black Horse pub. This hostelry, known for most of the 19th century as the Wild Horse, was kept by successive generations of the Habberton family.

▲ **HOLKHAM,** *The Village 1950* H340045

Substantially rebuilt by the Earl of Leicester in the 1880s, the village provides homes and a community for his staff. The far right building was the Reading Room; today it is the social club. The obelisk is a memorial erected by the 3rd Earl in memory of the nineteen Holkham men (including his younger son) who fell in the First World War.

◄ **HOLKHAM**
The Beach 1950 H340047

The beach is an area of outstanding natural beauty, and the dunes form a National Nature Reserve. Backed with a wind-break of Corsica pine planted by Thomas William Coke in the mid 19th century, this area is a breeding ground for birds such as terns, redshank and oystercatchers.

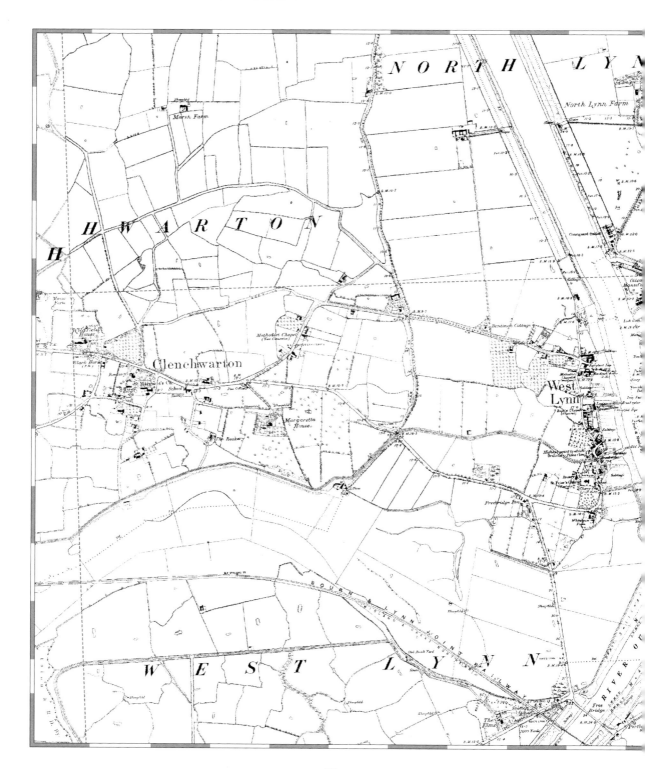

WELLS TO WEYBOURNE

WELLS-NEXT-THE-SEA, *The Beach House 1929* 81994

This was originally built as stabling for the gentry who would trot up the mile of embankment in their carriages to visit Wells beach. The Beach House soon became a refreshment rooms, and even had swing boats erected beside it. Despite extensive damage in the 1953 floods, a small café and shop still stands on the site.

38

WELLS-NEXT-THE-SEA
High Street 1929 82005

This scene is still recognisable today, but most of the shops in this area, like the London Central Meat Company (right), Thomas Harris the draper's and Edward Richford the newsagent's are long gone, and have been replaced by a local supermarket, restaurants and tourist shops.

WELLS-NEXT-THE-SEA, *The Motor Lifeboat and Tractor 1939* W48001

This 32-foot 'Surf' class lifeboat was the first RNLI boat to be propelled by Hotchkiss Cone engines. These worked on the principal of water-jet propulsion, and enabled the lifeboat to operate in shallow waters. Christened 'Royal Silver Jubilee 1910-1935', she cost £2,919, and served Wells between 1936 and 1945.

WELLS-NEXT-THE-SEA
The Beach 1939 W48005

Wells is pictured here in the days before flood and tempest smashed most of the beach huts to smithereens. The simple pleasures and uncrowded beach typify the beach in the time before most people had motor cars and there was still wide open spaces there, even in the height of summer.

WELLS-NEXT-THE-SEA, *The Beach 1939* W48007

Although Wells is a natural seaside resort with a soft sandy beach and shallow sea for bathing, the lookout and lifeboat station in the background mark the possibility of dangers, particularly for those who would ignore the signs and walk out across the shallows and flats when the tide was on the turn.

WELLS-NEXT-THE-SEA, *Jacob's Ladder 1950* W48051

When the Earl of Leicester made the embankment in the 19th century, he also planted the vast line of Corsica pines to stabilise the dunes from Holkham to Wells. These dunes were banked up to stop sea encroachments, and this set of steps had to be erected to enable access to the beach.

41

WELLS-NEXT-THE-SEA
The Boating Lake 1939
W48009

This beautiful area, known as Abraham's Bosom, was a superb boating lake surrounded by a belt of spruce and Corsica pines; it was one of the most popular destinations for young folk visiting Wells with their family in the 1930s. Sad to say, this whole area was severely damaged in the 1953 floods, and it has taken many years to re-create it.

WELLS-NEXT-THE-SEA, *The Embankment 1950* W48032

The one mile embankment was constructed in 1859 by the Earl of Leicester to enable the larger trading vessels to reach the town quayside. In the foreground is the memorial to the ten crewman of the lifeboat 'Eliza Adams', which capsized during a rescue in the great gale of 29 October 1880.

▲ **WELLS-NEXT-THE-SEA**
The Quay c1955 W48036

This was originally constructed in stone in 1853 as a 250-yard-long working quayside for vessels trading in barley, linseed cake, corn, timber, salt, malt and manure, rather than for holidaymakers. Wells quay is made unmistakable by the granary and gantry built for F & G Smith, the maltsters, in 1906. Today this building has become exclusive apartments and flats.

◄ **WELLS-NEXT-THE-SEA**
The Quay c1955 (detail) W48036

▼ WELLS-NEXT-THE-SEA, *The East End c1955* W48098

To the left in the middle distance we can see the gable end of the old Bullard's pub, the Shipwright's Arms. Although the pub may be gone, the building on the corner of the road has become a chandler's and boat yard for recreational sailors.

► WELLS-NEXT-THE-SEA
Staithe Street c1965
W48105

This street was pictured when the shops were more of a practical nature and suitable for a small town. Most of them are no more, and have been replaced by more tourist-orientated businesses, including tea rooms and gift shops. However, many of the new businesses are of good quality and very welcoming; as a result, this street is now busy with visitors for most of the year.

WELLS-NEXT-THE-SEA
Staithe Street c1965
W48144

Although the fashions may change, and businesses come and go, this view of Staithe Street is still easily recognisable today. On the left is Pechey & Son, a newsagent's and tobacconist's; although now part of a chain, it is still a newsagent today.

WELLS-NEXT-THE-SEA
Red Lion Yard 1950 W48049

This yard is typical of the long rows of houses and narrow roads built on the declivity towards the harbour in the town; many of the houses typically feature dormer windows in their roofs. Today most of the houses on the left have gone, while those on the right have been smartened up and are used as private residences.

45

WELLS-NEXT-THE-SEA ▶
The Quay Side c1965
W48134

Here we see the quay during the last years of Wells as a trading port. Large boats such as the 'Luctor' (centre right) were once familiar sights here. The railway line extended to the quay so that coal trucks could be loaded directly from the coal ships. Today the town's fortunes are based on tourism, and even the railway is no more.

◀ **BLAKENEY**
The Quay Side 1925
77524

When this photograph was taken, Blakeney was still a small trading port; it could accommodate vessels of 150 tons burden to unload and load coal, oil-cake and manure at the quay. Little or no mention of the village was made in the tourist guides at the time.

◄ **BLAKENEY**
The Church 1925 77528

Set on the high ground about
115ft above sea level, inland from
the main village, St Nicholas's
Church was erected and enlarged
from the 13th century by the
medieval wool traders of the area.
The smaller tower at the north-
east angle of the chancel was
erected by these same merchants
so that a lantern light could be
placed in it for the guidance of
their ships into the quay.

▶ **BLAKENEY**
The Quay c1955
B121045

Blakeney only really began to become popular as a tourist and holiday destination from the mid 1920s. At that time a number of old buildings were cleared from the quayside and the Blakeney Hotel (seen spreading along the quay to the right of the photograph) was built for the sum of £31,000—a huge investment in its day.

◀ **BLAKENEY**
The Harbour from the High Street c1965 B121166

This view shows the winding channel of some 4 miles between the open sea and the quayside. Its accompanying embankment was built to its present state in November 1897 after the 'Black Monday' storm severely damaged the old one. This 19th-century embankment has held well despite sporadic flood damage.

▲ **BLAKENEY,** *High Street c1965* B121127

In this area there are a concentration of attractive small plaques above the doors and lintels announcing that the cottages are owned by Blakeney Neighbourhood Housing Association. Founded by Nora Clogstoun in 1946, the association is not just concerned with the preservation of these beautiful homes; its primary purpose is to provide affordable homes to rent for local people.

◀ **MORSTON**
The Village c1955
M248061

This corner, just before the Anchor public house, is still familiar to any coast road traveller. On the right the houses still offer boat trips up the nearby creek to Blakeney Point. When in season, the locally harvested mussels sold here are outstanding for their size and flavour.

▼ **CLEY-NEXT-THE SEA,** *The Church c1955* C118001

St Margaret's stands on high ground at the southern end of the present village near the green at Newgate. The church was built in the 13th century and enlarged by wealthy Glaven port traders in the 14th century; the features, details and monuments inside are truly outstanding, even among the great wealth of medieval churches Norfolk is blessed with.

► **CLEY-NEXT-THE SEA**
The Mill c1955 C118006

Cley Mill is quite probably the most photographed image of the North Norfolk coast. It was erected in the early 19th century and was worked by successive generations of the Burroughes family until 1921, when it was sold for £350. It has since been converted into a dwelling and holiday home.

CLEY-NEXT-THE SEA
Wells Road c1955
C118014

The old forge on the left, with its distinctive cannon bosses sunk in front, is looking tired and rather sad. Luckily, in the 1970s the passing tourist trade encouraged it to be restored, along with several other properties in the village. The Forge became an art and craft shop. Today it is a superb delicatessen, but pottery and art shops may still be found in this delightful village today.

CLEY-NEXT-THE SEA
The Marshes c1955
C118026

The marshes were a popular haunt of wildfowlers seeking tasty birds and unusual specimens for the taxidermist. About 400 acres of this area were purchased by Dr Sydney Long in 1926. He believed the birds could be best appreciated alive and in their own habitat. He went on to found the Norfolk Wildlife Trust, and this became the first County Nature Reserve in the country.

► **SALTHOUSE**
The Creek c1955 S507027

This little pool fills up with all manner of water fowl; it has become a popular stopping-off place for coast road travellers, who feed the ducks and have an ice cream from the van parked there in the summer months.

◄ **SALTHOUSE**
*The Coast Road and
the Village Green c1955*
S507008

The village and salt marshes
here have had an uneasy
relationship over the years.
In 1851 about 500 acres of
marsh in the village and
adjoining parishes were
drained, but in the 1860s
the banks were broken and
never properly repaired.
The resultant creeks are
picturesque, but wise locals
keep sandbags ready in the
event of seasonal flooding.

▲ **SALTHOUSE**
The Post Office c1960 S507032

This vital hub of the village was run for years by the Star family. They not only provided the post office, but also newspapers and the posters outside kept the locals abreast of events both national and local; sweets, chocolates, tinned foods, candles and basic hardware could all be bought here. With the passing holiday trade in mind they also offered ices, a small café and the only petrol pump in the village!

▶ **SALTHOUSE**
The Post Office c1960 (detail)
S507032

SALTHOUSE
The Dun Cow c1955
S507031

The proprietors of the Broads and marshes as well as the Salthouse Stock and Cattle Association met here. The sturdy flint wall which curves around from the pub and along the coast road was built with their interests and high tides in mind. The cattle from the marshes could be brought into this enclosure if flooding threatened.

SALTHOUSE, *The Village and the Church 1955* S507016

The parish of Salthouse extends over 1,559 acres of land, 15 of water and 31 of foreshore. On a declivity towards the sea, the highest ground is occupied by the church of St Nicholas, rebuilt in the late 16th century by Sir Henry Heydon.

STIFFKEY
The AA Camp c1955 S193015

The Stiffkey Anti-Aircraft training camp was erected as a satellite
to the larger AA camp at Weybourne in the late 1930s. Throughout
the war, and for most of the National Service years, thousands of
soldiers passed through here. Today just a few brick ruins mark
the existence of the camp.

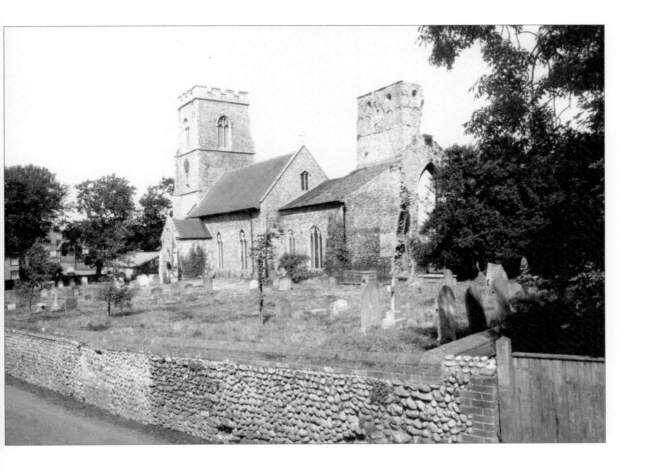

WEYBOURNE
The Church c1955 W353036

The Church of All Saints and the ruins of the priory dedicated
to the Blessed Virgin and All Saints are closely interwoven.
The original church was Saxon. The priory was erected in
the 13th century by Sir Ralph Manwaring, and occupied by
Augustinian canons subordinate to Westacre Priory.
The priory was dissolved by Henry VIII and given to
Richard Heydon in 1545.

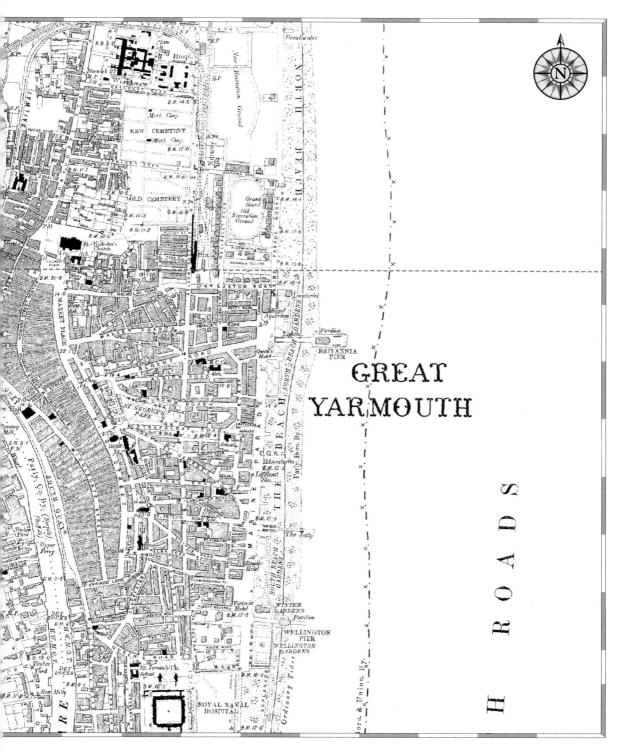

POPPYLAND:
UPPER SHERINGHAM
TO MUNDESLEY

UPPER SHERINGHAM, *The Parish Church 1894* 33317

The Church of All Saints is mainly 14th-century, and contains several fine tombs of the Upcher family. The bench ends are remarkable; they include a baby in swaddling clothes, Nebuchadnezzar eating grass, and even a mermaid, which is said to be modelled from life from a mermaid who would creep ashore and listen to the congregation singing from the north door.

SHERINGHAM
The Grand Hotel 1901
46543

The Grand, the Burlington and the Sheringham hotels were all built in the 1890s as high-class hotels for gentlefolk on their seaside holidays. After being used as troop quarters in the Second World War, the depressed holiday trade saw this great hotel converted into flats. Falling into tragic decay, it was demolished in 1974.

SHERINGHAM, *High Street c1955* S116036

Many of the businesses seen here may be gone, but they are still remembered with affection by older residents. Rust's the draper's and milliner's display the latest ladies' fashions, and next door Jordan's the chemist's had their scales outside— you could check your weight for a ha'penny (the chemist's is still going today). Next door again was the bakery run by Mr George High.

SHERINGHAM, *High Street 1921* 70993c

Centre stage is the distinctive frontage of Rust's, the draper's and milliner's that served generations of Sheringham ladies. The water all over the road undoubtedly comes from an overflow of the drinking troughs of 'Mary Pym', the nearby spring water well; it was canopied in 1862, and so nicknamed by locals after the lady who installed the clock on top of it in 1903.

SHERINGHAM
West Causeway c1955
S116016

The first promenades and sea defences at Sheringham were begun when it first became popular in the late 19th century. By 1900 the sea wall and promenade stretched for two-thirds of a mile. After the 1912 floods, a raised promenade and shelter were also constructed.

WEST RUNTON, *The Links Hotel and The Golf Club 1923* 74216

Pictured from the first tee of the course, the Runton Links Hotel was built in 1890. It was named after the renowned links designed by the champion Open golfer J H Taylor. A total of 6,125 yards in length, it was hailed as 'one of the most sporting golf courses in England.'

▼ **WEST RUNTON,** *Roseberry Road 1923* 74218

West Runton was a sleepy village until Cromer and Sheringham began to be popularised as holiday resorts. After the First World War it was hoped that the village would enjoy a greater expansion as a holiday resort. Built with the guesthouse trade in mind, most of these houses actually became homes. Runton's population doubled between 1890 and 1930.

▶ **WEST RUNTON**
The Shops 1923 74219

Newly built and ideally situated on the coast road, these shops (from the left George May's the stationer's, Phillips's hardware and groceries, and Mrs Harriet Lusher's bakery) were aimed at passing trade, and anticipated the expansion of West Runton as a holiday resort.

WEST RUNTON
The Beach 1925 77536

Many of the holidaymakers
seen here would undoubtedly
have chosen to follow the
new vogue to stay under the
canvas of a tent, rather than
to stay in guest houses or
hotels. A number of the cliff-
top fields around Runton Gap
were converted to camping
sites at this time.

WEST RUNTON
The Church c1955
W70107

The Church of the
Holy Trinity is a sturdy
14th-century building
with a 13th-century
western tower. In 1886
the tower and nave
roof were restored,
choir stalls were
placed in the chancel,
and the lychgate was
erected. In 1920 a new
roof was placed on the
south aisle and the old
lead recast for a total
cost of £500.

▶ **EAST RUNTON**
The Beach Entrance
1921 70968

East Runton cliffs were
noted for their unusual
'contorted' strata containing
huge masses of chalk. Most
folk, however, came to enjoy
the beach, which offered
the simple charms of beach
huts and occasional donkey
rides, and was far less
crowded than its neighbours
at Cromer and Sheringham.

◀ **EAST RUNTON**
The Gap c1955 E11034

By the 1950s, East Runton
was an established holiday
destination for campers
and caravaners. The old
Gap, originally used by
fishermen to reach the
sea, had become widened
by thousands of visitors'
feet, so it was smartened
up with ornamental
embankments by the
camp sites; even a café
was erected on the slope
of the Gap.

▲ **EAST RUNTON,** *The High Street c1955* E11009

Once Cromer and Sheringham became popular as holiday destinations, the Runtons (the villages between the towns) enjoyed the benefits of the overflowing holiday trade. From the early 20th century, two- or three-storey properties were erected as guest houses, some also containing shops. Such developments were undreamt of by locals in these sleepy fishing hamlets a generation before.

◄ **EAST RUNTON**
The Village Green c1955
E11048

A short distance from the coast road, modern village developments and camp sites many be found near East Runton Green or Lower Common. Here the rural charm of the village still exists, complete with duck pond and beautiful flint cottages, some of which date back to the 17th century.

CROMER
The East Beach 1901
46517

On the cliff top are the unmistakable domes of the Hotel de Paris, while behind the Bath House is the Hotel Metropole (now demolished). By the promenade at the bottom of the Gangway are the bathing machines (left); these were once pulled by ponies to the water's edge, where gentlefolk could step into the waters and not be seen in their bathing suits!

CROMER, *The View from Lighthouse Hill 1894* 33324

Cromer was one of the most fashionable resorts for gentlefolk in late Victorian Britain. The story of the town as a popular holiday destination began when the railway arrived in 1877. Most of the hotels and holiday apartments were only made possible after portions of the Cromer Hall estate were sold from the 1880s by Benjamin Bond Cabbell with the intention to develop Cromer as a seaside resort. Most of the buildings in the foreground were less than 10 years old when this photo was taken. To the right in the background, the old wooden jetty stretches out to sea. Partly washed away and severely damaged by a storm in 1897, it was replaced by the pier in 1901.

CROMER
The Marrams 1901
46523

The slopes and new esplanade that connected West Beach to East are almost completed, but still await their steep banks to be grassed and a railing to stop promenaders falling over the seaward side! On the right is the Marlborough Hotel, demolished after extensive damage caused by military occupation during the Second World War.

CROMER, *From the East Cliff 1906* 56849

Visitors beautifully attired in the finest Edwardian summer wear enjoy the cliff top promenade and the gentle slopes and steps down the cliff side. These walks were only made possible after the improvements of 1894-95 which removed the old narrow alleyways and steep steps; a contemporary guide said that they 'though picturesque, were trying'.

CROMER, *Jetty Street 1925* 78688

Originally named after its fine view overlooking the jetty, this street retained its name when the pier was built. This was possibly not just for nostalgia's sake, but also because of the number of houses here with jettied bay windows, which afford commanding views of the sea from their upper rooms.

CROMER
From the East Cliff
1933 85774

After the extensive investment of thousands of pounds, by the 1930s Cromer offered a sea wall, well-made promenades, and upper and lower parades complete with bastions and shelters. It was estimated that a walk of about a mile could be strolled along their length.

CROMER, *The East Beach c1955* C192017

With large trips to the seaside organised by youth groups, it was always a challenge to find different ways of entertaining large numbers of youngsters on the beach. Inspired by sand sculpture artists, the children are seen here competing for a sand drawing competition.

► **CROMER**
The Pier c1950 C192002

Fully restored after having its middle blown out as an anti-invasion measure in 1940, the pier has been returned to its true purpose of entertaining visitors. At the pier head is the Pavilion Theatre. With allowances for wars and disasters, the pier is home to the oldest end-of-the-pier summer show in England—its roots go back to 1921.

◄ **CROMER**
The Lifeboat c1948
C192021

The 'Millie Walton' was sent to Cromer for evaluation in 1945 before she was sent to her station on the Isle of Man. The crew were so impressed that they requested that they be allowed to keep her. Their wish was granted. The lifeboat was renamed the 'Henry Blogg' in 1948, and the great lifeboatman's nephew, Henry 'Shrimp' Davies, was Coxswain for the rest of her service.

▲ **CROMER,** *The Golf Links 1921* 70946

The Royal Cromer Golf Club was formed in 1887 with HRH Edward, Prince of Wales (later Edward VII) as its first Patron. The course of 6,200 yards was originally planned by Tom Morris, and later re-arranged and improved by Messrs Colt and Taylor. In 1921 gentlemen paid 5s a day, 7s 6d on Sundays, and 25s for a weekly ticket.

◄ **CROMER**
The Lighthouse 1933
85796

Built in 1832 in anticipation of the old lighthouse being lost in a cliff fall (which occurred in 1866), it was originally lit by oil lamps. It was converted to gas, and then fitted with electricity in 1936; the resultant 49,000 candle power beam could be seen up to 23 miles out to sea.

OVERSTRAND
*The Churches Old
and New 1891* 28751

St Martin's Church (right)
fell into ruin and was half
bricked up about 1750.
As new wealth came to
the area in the mid 19th
century, Christ Church
(left) was erected and
dedicated in 1867. In 1911,
St Martin's was restored
and re-opened and poor
Christ Church was left to
decay—no real evidence
of it remains today.

OVERSTRAND, *The High Street 1938* 88554

Known as the village of millionaires at the turn of the century (because no less than six lived in the village), Overstrand
maintained its exclusivity for many years. Despite a fine beach and a railway link, only a handful of hotels and guesthouses
could be found here. Pictured on the corner of the high street is the Engadine private hotel, run at the time by Mrs E G Edwards.

OVERSTRAND
The Sea Marge Hotel c1955
O31023

Sea Marge was built in the early 20th century as a private home for Sir Edgar Speyer, a German banker and reputed millionaire. He left Overstrand on the eve of war in 1914, and the building was soon converted to a hotel. Winston Churchill had a retreat here known as Pear Tree Cottage; it had no telephone, and it is said that it was to the Sea Marge that Churchill, when First Lord of the Admiralty, came to use their telephone in order to mobilise the British Fleet in 1914. After the war the hotel became a residential home; after extensive renovation, this historic building re-opened as a hotel in 1996.

OVERSTRAND, *The Cliff Café c1955* O31124

In the 1950s, Great British holidays enjoyed a revival. The pre-Beeching Act railways meant that people were able to visit a vast array of holiday destinations. Many of the little villages like Overstrand invested well by turning the old shed shops and tin cafes into modern premises. The Cliff Café is a fine example, photographed shortly after its refurbishment.

▼ **SIDESTRAND,** *The Church 1938* 88540

As the encroachments of the sea approached the old Sidestrand Church, it was decided to move it further inland; this church, built of as many as possible of the old church materials, was the result. It was opened in 1881. The old church tower, along with the old graves, was left on the cliff top. This area caught the imagination of Clement Scott, who waxed lyrical over this tranquil place, calling it 'Poppyland' in his writings for Daily Telegraph. His evocative word pictures saw visitors, including many leading aesthetes and theatre personalities, come by the trainload to the area.

▶ **TRIMINGHAM**
The Church c1955 T226007

The Church of St John the Baptist dates from the 13th century, with 14th- and 15th-century additions. The medieval priests here claimed to own the head of John the Baptist, and wonders were ascribed to it. It is safe to say that it probably was not the real head, but a realistic one of alabaster set up as object of devotion.

◄ TRIMINGHAM
Cromer Road c1955
T226014

Just up the road is the Crown & Anchor Hotel, kept in the 1930s by George William Risebrow. Offering garaging and a bowling green in 1937, he provided bed and breakfast from 4s 6d a night. After years of dereliction, the old hotel has now been restored as a private home.

MUNDESLEY
The Beach 1921
71009

Two routes are to be seen in the background leading to the beach. To the right, the private steps (now lost) from the Manor Hotel led to their own promenade. At the top of the public slope on the left may be seen the old Coastguard Station demolished in 1928 ; it was replaced by the building occupied today as a Coastwatch Station and museum.

▲ **MUNDESLEY**
The Beach c1955 M109042

Recovering nicely after the 1953 floods,
new huts on the promenade replace the
old ones which stood on the beach and
were smashed up in the storm along
with the original Beach Cafe. Its wooden
substitute was eventually replaced with
the concrete structure on tall columns—
that should keep the waters out!

▶ **MUNDESLEY**
The Beach c1955 (detail) M109042

MUNDESLEY
The Sands c1960
M109087

Seaside trips as I remember them! Good old British summers often seemed to have a keen breeze, and the vogue in the 1960s and 70s seemed to be more for a full pack hike to the beach carrying windbreak, cricket set, deck chairs and fully laden picnic hamper. Somebody always forgot the mallet!

MUNDESLEY, *The Post Office c1955* M109049

Originally built as an estate office for Thomas Wakeling, this building eventually became the permanent home of Mundesley Post Office in 1910. The sub-postmaster was none other than Norton T Wakeling, son of Thomas, who erected the building some years earlier. Norton remained, literally, in post for 40 years.

MUNDESLEY
High Street 1921 71010

This evocative image captures the atmosphere of Mundesley in the early 1920s. It is still recognisable today, but Percy Bladon Dando does not have his general store on the left any more. The road here is not made up with tarmac, nor are there any pavements—but judging from the look of the road, the most common traffic here is a pony and trap.

▶ **MUNDESLEY**
The Fisherman's Gangway c1955
M109035

Originally a rough roadway through the cliffs to the beach known as Cart Gap, the Gangway was constructed in concrete in 1898 by Steward & Patteson brewery, the owners of the Ship Hotel. Their actions were stirred to protect their property after a stormy sea smashed away most of the adjacent Lifeboat Hotel and cliff in 1897.

▼ **MUNDESLEY**
Kiln Cliffs Camping Site c1955
M109031

After the railway came to Mundesley in 1898, it was anticipated that the village would be as popular as Cromer. New properties and hotels were erected at such a pace that two brickyards were established. The boom did not come, and building stopped. It is somewhat ironic that the site along the west cliff where the holiday developments were planned became this caravan site.

▶ **MUNDESLEY**
The Parade c1960
M109068

This short parade was built about 1905 and originally contained three businesses: a newsagent and lending library, a draper's, and a tea room. The little newsagent's was always renowned for a fine range of souvenirs, especially a nice line in china. It was also from here that thousands of postcards were purchased to tell all at home about their stay.

◄ **MUNDESLEY**
The Ship Hotel
c1955 M109065

The Ship was described as one of the 'three good inns' of Mundesley in 1845. Among the facilities offered by the hotel were a quoits bed and bowling green. The problem was its proximity to the cliff edge. Concerns were aroused after a number of incidents where bowls fell over the cliff and narrowly missed people on the beach below.

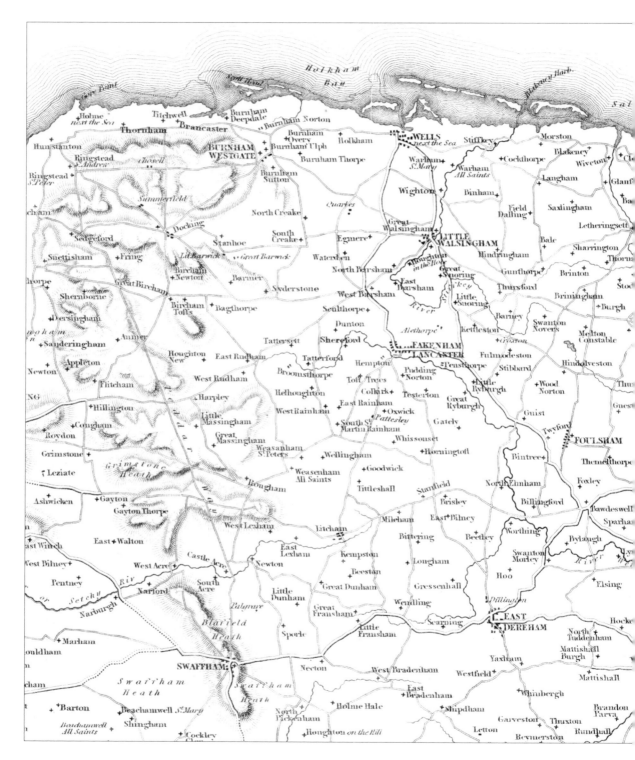

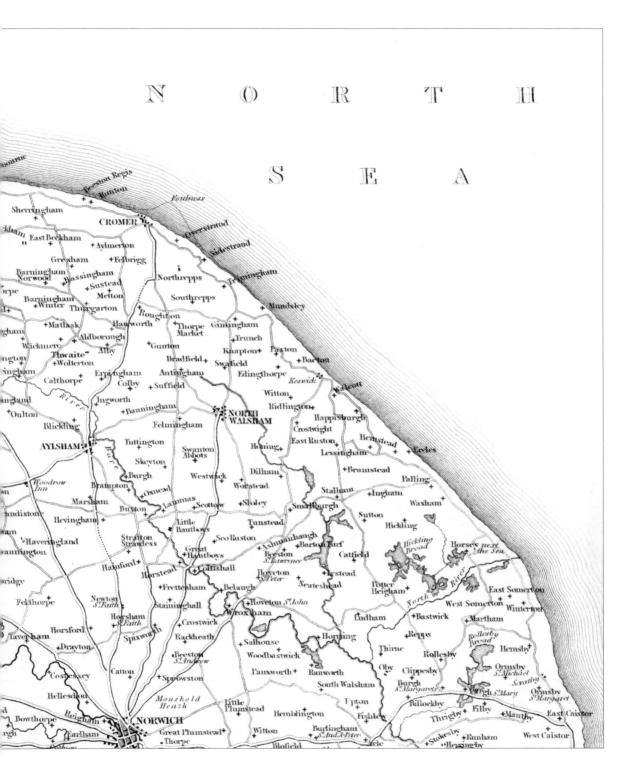

PASTON
TO GREAT
YARMOUTH
AND
GORLESTON

PASTON
Stow Mill c1960 M109084

Built by James Gaze in 1827, Stow Mill passed to his son Thomas the following year—he worked it until his death in 1872. The business was carried on by his son William until 1906, when it was sold to Mrs Harper and her cousin Thomas Livermore, who worked the mill until it ceased to operate in 1930. After a number of years of neglect, it was restored to former glory in the 1970s and is now open to the public.

▶ **PASTON**
The Tithe Barn c1965
P248013

Built in 1581 for the Paston family, this is the only complete structure from the Paston estate still standing. Constructed by the same craftsmen that built Trunch and Knapton churches, the barn is,160ft long, 24ft wide and about 60ft from floor to roof apex. Its historical significance is beyond question, and its restoration and maintenance is an ongoing process.

◄ **BACTON**
Sea View Café c1955
B493018

Up to the Second World War, Bacton remained a sleepy fishing hamlet. In the late 1940s and early 50s caravan and camping sites saw the village embrace the holiday trade with an amusement arcade and new shops like Sea View Café, which were conveniently sited near the beach for visitors staying on the campsites away from the village centre.

▼ **BACTON,** *The Abbey 1933* 85862

Properly titled Bromholm Priory, this was a Cluniac priory, founded in 1113 by William de Glanville. It was well known that the priory had a miraculous section of the True Cross, and a popular exclamation in 14th- and 15th-century texts was 'Oh, Holy Rood of Bromholm!' The religious house fell at the Dissolution in 1536, and only a few ruins hint at its glory today.

► **HAPPISBURGH**
North Walsham Road
c1965 H304009

On the left is the 110ft tower of St Mary's Church. The other building standing proud on the horizon is Hill House. This fine old pub was visited by Sir Arthur Conan Doyle in 1903. The son of innkeeper, Mr Cubitt, had his own pictogram code; this fascinated Doyle to such a degree that he used it in his Sherlock Holmes story 'The Dancing Men'.

HAPPISBURGH
The Caravan Site and the Church
c1965 H304077

This is still a caravan site today. The embanked pathway has now been flattened and the roadway resurfaced. In the centre of the photograph is a railway signal box built in 1901 for the planned extension of the line from Mundesley to Stalham. The tracks never came, and the box has only been used for holiday accommodation.

HAPPISBURGH
Wayside Stores
c1965 H304110

This little store and village post office is well remembered for being run for many years by the Moody family. Although the shop area is a little smaller, it is still going today. Adjacent to the store is the village school erected in 1861 for 120 local children. A full pavement was only introduced to this street in 1979.

HAPPISBURGH
Cliff Bungalows c1955
H304017

Happisburgh has drawn
national press attention for the
way the sea has claimed land
in this area. These bungalows,
which commanded such
magnificent sea views, have
now toppled over the cliff edge.
The roadway here, known as
'the cinder track', now teeters
precariously on the cliff top.

HAPPISBURGH, *Dogers Point c1955* H304015

This area has always been of danger to shipping. Such was the concern in 1791, that two beacons were erected, illuminated
by lanterns holding many candles; one became the lighthouse, and another stood about 400 yards north of Cart Gap. Known
as the high light and low light, they saved many a vessel traversing the infamous Haisbro' Sands.

HAPPISBURGH
The Lighthouse c1965 H304008

The lighthouse was built in 1791, and an occulting light and the famous red stripes were added in 1883. Changed to electricity in 1942, the lighthouse was eventually given up by Trinity House in 1987. A private Act of Parliament was brought by locals to save it, and today, beautifully restored, the lighthouse is maintained by a trust who have been granted a 99-year lease.

93

▶ **SEA PALLING**
The Beach Restaurant
c1950 S470011

The village of Sea Palling was changed irrevocably by the east coast floods of 1953. Most of the buildings behind and beside this restaurant took the brunt of the assault when the water breached the gap in the dunes, and were wrecked. The Beach Restaurant was a remarkable survivor, but it suffered extensive flood damage.

◀ **SEA PALLING**
The Lifeboat Tavern
c1955 S470039

The original Two Lifeboats pub was torn apart by the 1953 floods. This new tavern was built in replacement. The veranda has now been enclosed by French windows. A good pint or a meal may still be had at the renamed Reef's Bar.

▲ **SEA PALLING,** *The Village c1950* S470036

This view from Mill Lane has changed little, but the methods of harvesting the fields are worlds apart. The hay has been left to dry, and was no doubt turned before making the stooks lined up like Indian tepees along the field. These would be used to make a haystack with a thatched top, just like the one in the background.

◄ **HORSEY**
The Street c1955 H341006

Little has changed here. Street Farm (left) still displays parish notices, and the sign (far right) still directs travellers to the excellent Nelson Head pub. The barn just up the road was erected in 1742; despite its being in a poor condition today, efforts are being made to restore it for use as a dwelling.

95

▼ **HORSEY,** *The Village c1955* H341007

The small area of ground in the fork in the road was donated to the village by Major Anthony Buxton DSO, JP of Horsey Hall. Pleasantly grassed and surrounded by fragrant shrubs, it is a delightful place of peace which can be enjoyed while sitting on the bench erected in memory of the good Major.

▶ **HORSEY**
The Mill c1955 H341018

Constructed by Dan England in 1912, this drainage mill has done sterling work during various floods over the years. Struck by lightening in 1943, the old mill was left to rot until it was restored by the County Council in the 1960s. Today thousands every year visit the mill and the mere, a designated site of specific scientific interest and a special protection area for birds.

WINTERTON
The Church c1960
W357095

Holy Trinity and All Saints' Church was built about 1400 and has a 132ft tower. Inside the church is an interesting fishermen's memorial chapel made and decorated with wood from locally wrecked ships. This view of the church from Black Street has now irrevocably changed with a number of bungalows erected along this country lane.

WINTERTON
The Beach c1955
W357020

Up to the Second World War about 250 people from the village were employed in the herring and mackerel industry. From the late 1940s, the emphasis of business turned towards tourism. The excellent sands were discovered by more and more families who appreciated the attractions here—Winterton was less commercial or brash than its coastal neighbours.

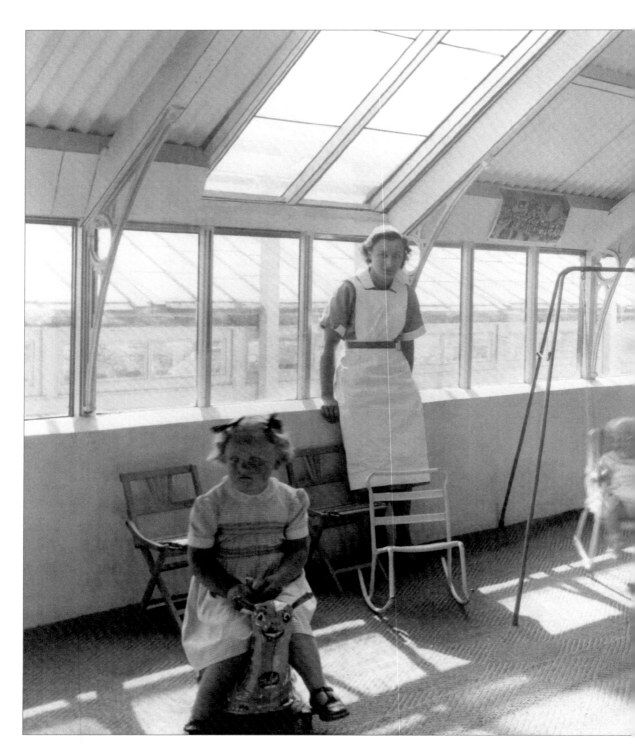

WINTERTON
*The Chalet Hotel and
Country Club,
The Nursery c1955*
W357059

When the holiday trade
developed, the Chalet
Hotel sprang up; it offered
accommodation and
entertainment for all
the family. The complex
eventually took over the old
coastguard buildings and even
the redundant lighthouse.

▼ **HEMSBY,** *The Beach c1965* H306111

In the 1960s Hemsby found its feet as a popular haven for holidaymakers. It was during this time that most of the wooden cottages and shops along Beach Road became the concrete amusements and shops we know today.

► **HEMSBY**
The Donkeys c1955
H306068

Donkeys are among the most placid and understanding of animals. Be it shouts, bumping in the saddle, or sticky fingers in the mane, these donkeys would plod their way up and down the beach, and little would alarm them. By the 1950s, donkey rides and derbys were part of the standard seaside fare at every resort; today, health and safety regulations and astronomical insurance cover prices for owners have made them a thing of the past.

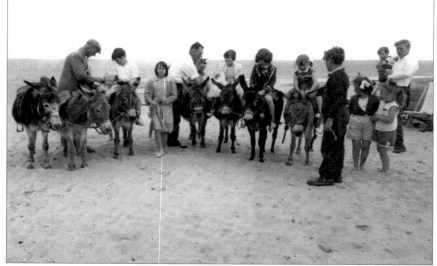

◄ HEMSBY
The Lacon Arms
c1955 H306060

The Lacon Arms opened in 1934, when the first holiday developments were being erected in the village; thousands of 'swift pints' have been downed here over the years. Tragedy struck the pub in 1970 when a fire gutted the building. Restored to former glory, the pub is till open today—although after the major fire, tiles rather than thatch now adorn the roof.

HEMSBY
St Mary's Church c1955
H306064

Away from the tourist area of Beach Road the little village of Hemsby remained unspoilt for many years. Still standing without change is St Mary's. Dating from the mid 15th century it was extensively restored in 1866 at a cost of £1,200, mostly paid thanks to the benefaction of Mr Robert Copeman, many of whose ancestors are buried within its walls.

▼ **CAISTER-ON-SEA,** *The Church 1908* 60668

Holy Trinity Church, built in the Early English and Perpendicular styles, has a register dating back to 1563. After falling into disrepair, it was restored in 1894. The most poignant memorial in the church is the east window, erected in 1903 in memory of the nine men who 'never turned back' and lost their lives in the Caister Lifeboat disaster of 1901.

► **CAISTER-ON-SEA**
The Railway Station c1955
C450003

The railway first passed through Caister in 1877. In 1937 this halt was built at the holiday camp to allow the holiday camp expresses which ran from London to Yarmouth to drop off passengers. The line was closed in March 1959, and the tracks were taken up shortly afterwards. Today the site is occupied by private housing.

CAISTER-ON-SEA
The Lifeboat c1955
C450110

The 'Jose Neville' was the first motor lifeboat to serve at the Caister RNLI station. Between the years 1941 and 1964 she was launched on service 107 times, saving 75 lives. To the horror of local people, the RNLI closed the station in 1969. Today Caister Volunteer Rescue Service provides the same service as their brave forbears, and is entirely supported by voluntary donations.

CAISTER-ON-SEA
The Holiday Camp
c1955 C450137

In 1906, Fletcher Dodd began to provide holidays for groups of socialists from the East End of London in the grounds of his house on Ormesby Road. The potential of a holiday camp soon became apparent, and Dodd acquired nearby land which became the first holiday camp in England. Although the original 1906 site has been built on, the expanded camp site was bought by Ladbrokes in 1973 and is still going today.

GREAT YARMOUTH
The Beach 1899 44496

Always Norfolk's biggest and most
popular holiday resort, Great Yarmouth
always tried to find the latest attraction.
It was known for its pleasure beach, and
before the days of the scenic railway
visitors could get a bird's eye view of the
town from the Revolving Tower (left).
Built in 1897, it was 120ft high with a
cage capable of holding 150 people that
rotated as it went up and down. It was
just one of five in the whole country. The
tower was demolished in 1941 and the
metal sent for war salvage.

GREAT YARMOUTH
The Beach 1899 (detail) 44496

GREAT YARMOUTH
The New Britannia Pier 1902 49072

Originally built in 1858 for £6000, the Britannia Pier was rebuilt in 1901–02 with a new pavilion for £65,000. In 1910 the pavilion burnt down; a replacement was soon erected to seat 1,400 people. The Floral Hall also burnt down in 1932, but a new dance hall for 2,500 was built to replace it and opened the following year.

GREAT YARMOUTH, *The Promenade and the Beach 1894* 33386

The promenade is pictured in its late 19th century heyday. Promenaders are attired in the latest fashions, with no gentlemen being seen without his cane or umbrella. On the right is the seated enclosure for the Beach Concert Party, whose playbills offered 'a unique performance of songs, amusements, minstrels, magic and performing dogs!'

► **GREAT YARMOUTH**
*The Marina and
Britannia Pier c1955*
G56042

Victorian concert party
enclosures progressed
to concrete shelters and
rooftop walkways in the
1950s. Here such artists as
Waldini and his Orchestra
performed under banners
proclaiming 'Music with
a Smile'. This area, after
being occupied by a
Wild West show in the
late 1960s and early 70s,
is now occupied by the
Marina Centre indoor
swimming pool complex.

◄ **GREAT YARMOUTH**
Waterways c1960
G56071

In the 1960s the water
gardens with their smartly
trimmed lawns and rustic
bridges were enjoyed by
all ages. One of the fun
activities on a sunny day was
to cruise along these garden
waterways in one of the
ornamental motorboats. A
real treat was to come back
and take the same trip at
night when the gardens were
illuminated.

▲ **GREAT YARMOUTH,** *Blackfriars Tower 1891* 28710

This is one of fifteen towers built with the defensive walls of the town between 1284 and 1396. The Blackfriars, otherwise known as the South-East Tower, was used in the 19th century as a shop at street level with accommodation above—there was even a small cottage built on top. Today the modern additions have been removed, and the town wall and tower are revealed and restored.

◄ **GREAT YARMOUTH**
Wellington Pier c1955
G56036

This pier opened in 1854. It was acquired by the Corporation in 1900, and they rebuilt the pier with a pavilion and promenade in 1903. In the same year they purchased the glass Winter Garden from Torquay, dismantled it and erected it beside the pier entrance. From the 1950s some of the biggest names in entertainment, including Bob Monkhouse, Harry Secombe and Dick Emery, appeared at the pier.

GREAT YARMOUTH
The Market 1922 72526

The market has always done brisk trade, but it is most renowned for seafood and chips. Most of the shops on the right have been demolished or modernised, and the double tram track (laid in 1913) is long gone. Another loss is the spire on St Nicholas's Church (background right); after the church was bombed out in June 1942, the funds could not stretch to a spire when it was rebuilt.

▶ **GREAT YARMOUTH**
Anchor Gardens c1955
G56025

The gardens are named after
the great floral anchors that
adorned them. Here we are
given a fine view of some
of the Marine Parade guest
houses, including the Granby
and Ocean Spray. The Empire
cinema (centre) is showing
the film 'Tycoon.'

◀ **GORLESTON**
The Harbour 1894 33394

Seen here are some of over a thousand steam and sail drifters which operated out of Gorleston harbour during the herring season at the turn of the century. When this photograph was taken, considerable improvements were under way. Two lighthouses had been erected at the river mouth in 1887, and the fog bell, audible for 2 miles out to sea, was erected in 1895.

◄ **GORLESTON**
The Beach 1922 72537

Unlike many Norfolk beaches, which allowed the erection of permanent wooden beach huts, Gorleston offered a few temporary huts for weekly hire and a 'village' of square tents. At the turn of the century the lucrative tents were a closed shop run by number of families: the Dentons (Harry Denton was the bathing machine proprietor and port sanitary inspector), the Dyes and the Austrins.

◄ **GORLESTON**
The Beach 1908
60661

This is a fine view of the 'lost beach' of Gorleston, so named because after years of erosion it has been reduced to a fraction of the size we see here. In the background is the Pier Hotel, built in the 1890s on the site of the Anchor of Hope, the old fishermen's haunt.

◄ **GORLESTON**
The Beach and the Promenade 1922 72541

The Gorleston Pavilion (left), always a popular venue with its dance hall and theatre, is hosting the summer show—The Revumorists. In the centre of the photograph we can see the 64ft, red brick lighthouse on the Brush Wharf, built at a cost of £400.

GORLESTON
The Old Dutch Pier
c1965 G35008

We are looking across the 'Cosies'. It was here that many folks spent a happy day in the shelter of the 16th-century timbers of the original pier, fishing, reading, or just watching the ships go by. The Cosies were destroyed in 1964; they were inconsiderately stripped away when the pier was rebuilt and faced with concrete.

GORLESTON, *The Children's Yachting Lake c1960* G35015

The boating lake and nearby bathing pool were always popular attractions for holidaymakers and locals alike. Many local fishermen spent the lean time in the winter and summer evenings crafting detailed sailing boats to sell during the next summer season. Hotly contested competitions were fought, and it was a matter of pride to find who could craft and sail the best model.

INDEX

FRITH PRODUCTS & SERVICES

Francis Frith would doubtless be pleased to know that the pioneering publishing venture he started in 1860 still continues today. Over a hundred and forty years later, The Francis Frith Collection continues in the same innovative tradition and is now one of the foremost publishers of vintage photographs in the world. Some of the current activities include:

INTERIOR DECORATION

Today Frith's photographs can be seen framed and as giant wall murals in thousands of pubs, restaurants, hotels, banks, retail stores and other public buildings throughout the country. In every case they enhance the unique local atmosphere of the places they depict and provide reminders of gentler days in an increasingly busy and frenetic world.

PRODUCT PROMOTIONS

Frith products are used by many major companies to promote the sales of their own products or to reinforce their own history and heritage. Frith promotions have been used by Hovis bread, Courage beers, Scots Porage Oats, Colman's mustard, Cadbury's foods, Mellow Birds coffee, Dunhill pipe tobacco, Guinness, and Bulmer's Cider.

GENEALOGY AND FAMILY HISTORY

As the interest in family history and roots grows world-wide, more and more people are turning to Frith's photographs of Great Britain for images of the towns, villages and streets where their ancestors lived; and, of course, photographs of the churches and chapels where their ancestors were christened, married and buried are an essential part of every genealogy tree and family album.

FRITH PRODUCTS

All Frith photographs are available Framed or just as Mounted Prints and Posters (size 23 x 16 inches). These may be ordered from the address below. Other products available are - Address Books, Calendars, Jigsaws, Canvas Prints, Postcards and local and prestige books.

THE INTERNET

Already ninety thousand Frith photographs can be viewed and purchased on the internet through the Frith websites and a myriad of partner sites.

For more detailed information on Frith products, look at this site:
www.francisfrith.com

See the complete list of Frith Books at: www.francisfrith.com
This web site is regularly updated with the latest list of publications from The Francis Frith Collection. If you wish to buy books relating to another part of the country that your local bookshop does not stock, you may purchase on-line.

For further information, trade, or author enquiries please contact us at the address below:
The Francis Frith Collection, Unit 6, Oakley Business Park, Wylye Road, Dinton, Wiltshire SP3 5EU.
Tel: +44 (0)1722 716 376 Fax: +44 (0)1722 716 881 Email: sales@francisfrith.co.uk

---

See Frith products on the internet at www.francisfrith.com

FREE PRINT OF YOUR CHOICE

Mounted Print
Overall size 14 x 11 inches (355 x 280mm)

Choose any Frith photograph in this book.
Simply complete the Voucher opposite and
return it with your remittance for £3.50 (to cover
postage and handling) and we will print the
photograph of your choice in SEPIA (size 11 x 8
inches) and supply it in a cream mount with a
burgundy rule line (overall size 14 x 11 inches).
Please note: aerial photographs and
photographs with a reference number
starting with a "Z" are not Frith photographs
and cannot be supplied under this offer.
Offer valid for delivery to one UK address only.

**PLUS: Order additional Mounted Prints
at HALF PRICE - £10.00 each** (normally £20.00)
If you would like to order more Frith prints from
this book, possibly as gifts for friends and family,
you can buy them at half price (with no
additional postage and handling costs).

PLUS: Have your Mounted Prints framed
For an extra £19.00 per print you can have your
mounted print(s) framed in an elegant polished
wood and gilt moulding, overall size
16 x 13 inches (no additional postage and
handling required).

IMPORTANT!

**These special prices are only available if you use
this form to order. You must use the ORIGINAL
VOUCHER on this page (no copies permitted). We
can only despatch to one UK address. This offer
cannot be combined with any other offer.**

Send completed Voucher form to:
**The Francis Frith Collection, Unit 6,
Oakley Business Park, Wylye Road,
Dinton, Wiltshire SP3 5EU**

CHOOSE A PHOTOGRAPH FROM THIS BOOK

Voucher for **FREE** and Reduced Price Frith Prints

*Please do not photocopy this voucher. Only the original is valid,
so please fill it in, cut it out and return it to us with your order.*

Picture ref no	Page no	Qty	Mounted @ £10.00	Framed + £19.00	Total Cost £
		1	Free of charge*	£	£
			£10.00	£	£
			£10.00	£	£
			£10.00	£	£
			£10.00	£	£
			£10.00	£	£

*Please allow 28 days
for delivery.
Offer available to one
UK address only*

* Post & handling	£3.80
Total Order Cost	£

Title of this book . . . .
I enclose a cheque/postal order for £ . . . .
made payable to 'The Francis Frith Collection'

OR please debit my Mastercard / Visa / Maestro card,
details below

Card Number:

Issue No (Maestro only):   Valid from (Maestro):

Card Security Number: Expires:

Signature:

Name Mr/Mrs/Ms . . . .
Address . . . .
. . . .
. . . .
. . . . Postcode . . . .
Daytime Tel No . . . .
Email . . . .

Valid to 31/12/14

Can you help us with information about any of the Frith photographs in this book?

We are gradually compiling an historical record for each of the photographs in the Frith archive. It is always fascinating to find out the names of the people shown in the pictures, as well as insights into the shops, buildings and other features depicted.

If you recognize anyone in the photographs in this book, or if you have information not already included in the author's caption, do let us know. We would love to hear from you, and will try to publish it in future books or articles.

An Invitation from The Francis Frith Collection to Share Your Memories

The 'Share Your Memories' feature of our website allows members of the public to add personal memories relating to the places featured in our photographs, or comment on others already added. Seeing a place from your past can rekindle forgotten or long held memories. Why not visit the website, find photographs of places you know well and add YOUR story for others to read and enjoy? We would love to hear from you!

www.francisfrith.com/memories

Our production team

Frith books are produced by a small dedicated team at offices near Salisbury. Most have worked with the Frith Collection for many years. All have in common one quality: they have a passion for the Frith Collection.

Frith Books and Gifts

We have a wide range of books and gifts available on our website utilising our photographic archive, many of which can be individually personalised.

www.francisfrith.com

Free Print – see overleaf

Contains material sourced from responsibly managed forests.

FF007622